Walking the Narrow Road

The Wang Ming-Tao Story

Also by Brother David:

God's Smuggler to China, with Dan Wooding and Sara Bruce

Walking the Hard Road

The Wang Ming-Tao Story

by Brother David
with Sara Bruce and Lela Gilbert
in conjunction with Open Doors

Marshall Pickering

Marshall Morgan and Scott
Marshall Pickering
34 – 42 Cleveland Street, London, W1P 5FB, U.K.

Scripture quotations identified *KJV* are from the King James
Version of the Bible.
Scripture quotations identified *NAS* are from the New
American Standard Bible, copyright © The Lockman
Foundation 1961, 1962, 1963, 1968, 1971, 1972, 1973, 1975, 1977
and are used by permission.
Scripture quotations identified *NIV* are from the New
International Version, copyright © The Zondervan
Corporation, 1973, 1978, 1984 and 1985 and are used by
permission.

ISBN 0-551–01445–8
Wang Ming Tao : Walking the Hard Road.
  1. China — Church history — 20th century
  275.1 BR1288

Text set in Bembo by Selectmove Ltd
Printed in Great Britain
by Cox & Wyman Ltd, Reading

About the author

Brother David is an American missionary serving the Lord through the ministry of Open Doors with Brother Andrew, an organization that provides Bibles and other helps to the Church in the restricted countries of the world. He and his wife Julie have spent the past twenty-four years in Asia. He directed the Open Doors ministry to China and Asia for fifteen years. He is the author of the book *God's Smuggler to China*, which is published in more than twelve languages worldwide.*

Brother David is known for his ministry of encouragement and his love for the Church in Asia and particularly in China. He has a burning vision for China's one billion precious souls. He has a close relationship with most China ministries based in Hong Kong. Brother David is a close friend to Mr and Mrs Wang Ming-Tao, indeed a devoted friend to the Chinese Church across China. Today he is minister at large for Open Doors International.

* Brother David, with Dan Wooding and Sara Bruce, *God's Smuggler to China* (Hodder and Stoughton, London 1983).

Walking the Hard Road

Walking the Hard Road will take you down many paths in the life of my 'Uncle in Christ', Wang Ming-Tao. The book is divided into different parts, each one a road he has walked. All have a message for you and me. As we travel them, it is Wang Ming-Tao's prayer that you and I will choose to 'walk the hard road'.

Brother David

Note: Most publications today call him Wang Ming-Dao. During one of my visits with uncle he wrote his English signature on his foggy window – 'Wang Ming-Tao'.

'But as for me, I keep watch for the Lord, I wait in hope for God my Saviour; my God will hear me. Do not gloat over me, my enemy! Though I have fallen, I will rise. Though I sit in darkness, the Lord will be my light. Because I have sinned against him, I will bear the Lord's wrath, until he pleads my case and establishes my right. He will bring me out into the light; I will see his justice' (Micah 7.7–9 NIV).

Wang Ming-Tao
Shanghai, 1985

Contents

Acknowledgments

Section I

His Greeting

'All the way my Saviour leads me.'

1. New Friends

The Shanghai night was black with coal smoke. Our bus crawled among teeming traffic lanes, past dim orange street lights. The ageing brick residences lining the avenue had been built long before the Chinese Communist Revolution. We could barely read their address numerals as we rumbled past.

After glancing at the assortment of blue-clad passengers who crowded the bus, my eyes fell on my companions. Andy Wee and Stephen Lo were longtime, trusted colleagues. The three of us were on our way to a home that hosted house church meetings, and only Stephen knew the way. Suddenly his eye caught a number on a building. He motioned for us to disembark.

Brisk March winds cut through our bodies as we set out into the darkness. Any visit to the site of a Chinese house church always brings with it a certain tension. Such meetings have to be secret – risks for the Christians involved are very great. For this reason, we were surprised to be met by one of the believers.

Lin, host of the little fellowship, told us to be quiet and to follow him in the shadows of the old buildings. We walked several blocks, silently moving along. At last he made a right turn down an alley. Above our heads, clean laundry festooned the narrow passageway. After walking another twenty yards or so, Lin turned left abruptly.

At last we entered a simple, undecorated living room. There, like a warm tide, a wave of peace seemed to wash over us. When Ping, Lin's wife, and their two sons entered the room, we hesitated no longer. Our carefully-hidden cargo was immediately placed in their grateful, trembling hands – one hundred Bibles!

'It's a miracle . . .' Ping's husband shook his head in wonder. 'By last night our entire supply of Bibles had been distributed! And by now our Lord has wonderfully brought you here with more! Praise Him!'

The man took his new treasure into a rustic bedroom and hid it lovingly in an old trunk at the foot of his bed. When he returned to the living room, we began to pray and offer thanks to the Lord.

Displaying the matchless hospitality we have always experienced in Chinese homes, rich or poor, Ping excused herself long enough to bring us Chinese dumplings and scalding cups of tea. I began to feel a sense of urgency. We had a further task to pursue that night. When should I ask the question that stirred within me?

At last the conversation lulled. I took a breath. 'Do you know . . .' I began a little hesitantly, 'how we might meet Pastor and Mrs Wang Ming-Tao?'

Stephen studied Ping for a moment. 'We would very much like to meet him,' he told her. Ping nodded.

Ping seemed to be considering the situation carefully. At last she said, 'It would not be at all convenient for us to go there at the moment. However . . .' She weighed the possibilities. 'Would you be able to come back tomorrow at around two o'clock?'

Ping explained that it would be best to meet Wang and his wife at her place rather than at their own apartment. Ping had many relatives living in other countries. It would be more natural for her to entertain foreign guests in her home.

A definite meeting time was set, and a prayer of blessing was offered. We walked out to the main street to catch a bus. And as we walked our hearts were full of excitement and gratitude towards these friends and towards our Lord who had brought us all together.

As the bus found its way back to our hotel through Shanghai, a sense of anticipation surged within me. We rode along without speaking. *If the Lord makes that meeting possible*, I told myself, *we'll soon be in the presence of two of God's most precious servants*.

I could never have guessed that it would be the first of many such meetings. How could I have known that one day I would learn to call that courageous, heroic old man 'Uncle' and his radiant wife 'Aunty'?

Next afternoon, we returned to Lin's apartment. In the daylight, we had a better look at our surroundings. The streets of Shanghai bustled with traffic. Countless bicycles and buses mingled along the *bund*, the broad avenue that winds beside the busy harbour. European-style buildings rose majestically above the trees, looking for all the world as if they had been borrowed from a city on the other side of the globe.

Soon our bus turned down a narrower road. Rivers of dull-garbed workers streamed along the walkways. A broom-seller dozed among his straw wares, oblivious to the teeming crowds. Shoppers examined fatty hams and ribs in red-bannered state markets. The longer we rode, the older the buildings seemed to grow.

Past colourful markets and crooked-roofed houses we moved along until we stopped near Lin's humble dwelling and found our way inside. Once there, I looked around at the same room we had visited the night before. An old, empty fireplace sat clean and well-swept at one end of the room. In front of it were two brown unupholstered chairs.

At the other end of the room was a round antiquated table. A small lamp hung over it, its bulb exposed. There was no elegance to the place, except for the beauty that shone in the faces of the ten Christian believers who sat awaiting the arrival of Wang Ming-Tao and his wife.

It did not take us long to learn that half of them had spent, collectively speaking, a total of eighty years in Chinese prisons – simply for being Christian believers.

I looked at them with tears stinging my eyes. *I shouldn't even be in their presence! How can I talk to them? I've never been through the fire the way they have.*

For the half-hour or so that passed before the old man arrived, I listened to them talking. And I was amazed by what I learned. The night before, Ping had led in prayer as we were getting ready to leave. She had specifically asked that when we gathered again the next day, the Holy Spirit would bring together only the people He wanted to fellowship with Wang Ming-Tao. Now we found ourselves in the midst of a dozen people. And not one of them had known about the meeting!

Every person in that room had felt urged to go to Lin's that afternoon. They had simply wanted to visit! Now there they were, led by the Lord to meet with Wang and his wife, Debra. They had thought they might see us. But they had no idea they would be spending the afternoon with Wang Ming-Tao.

None of the believers present, however, were un-aware of who the old man was. He was legendary among these people. It was March, 1980. He had been out of prison only three months. Prior to that, he had been serving a 'life' sentence for twenty-two years and ten months.

At about three p.m. we heard a rustling outside. The pastor and his wife had arrived. Our eyes turned toward the door. And I will never forget the sight of those two faithful pilgrims.

It seemed as if two shining beams of light had suddenly burst through into the room. Their faces literally glowed as the glory of the Lord seemed to be radiating from their countenances.

The aged man's long face curved in a smile. The wisdom inscribed in his face suggested to me the beauty of a serene old owl. Grace and peace seemed to surround him.

Lord, I thought to myself, *I feel like I'm in the presence of your angels!*

16

One by one he greeted us. Pastor Wang made a point of getting to know each one of us. The questions were translated. 'Who are you? Where are you from?' Wang Ming-Tao was nearly blind. He came up to each of us and looked directly into our faces. His eyes seemed to pierce through our very souls.

It was soon evident that his hearing was weak. He wore a curious, ancient hearing-aid. It fitted onto his right ear and was connected by a cord to a little box. Now and then the volume would grow too loud. A shrill screech would fill the room.

By the time all the introductions were made, fourteen people were together. Ping invited the two elders to sit in the two old chairs by the fireplace. Then came the delightful dumplings and tea once again. And our fellowship really began.

I glanced around the room as the friendly chatter continued. Nearly everyone there wore faded blue Chinese clothing. All the ladies but one wore trousers. Their appearance reflected that of the crowds that surged in all of China's metropolitan areas. Almost everyone wore blue or green during that time. Today the picture is different – somewhat more colourful. Then, everyone needed to identify with the masses.

Interesting conversation, I thought to myself as Stephen Lo quietly interpreted what was being said. *In spite of the fact that all these people have been in prison, they've completely turned their attention to the old man. His story is all they care about. Not one of them is trying to call attention to himself.*

My mind wandered to the church social events I had often attended in the Western world. From time to time, I had heard competitive dialogues where one person would attempt to upstage another. Frequently, the older guests would fall silent at the outspoken words of the young. *It's certainly a different world* . . . I thought to myself. *There's so much to learn from the way these brethren give respect to the elderly.*

The sound of singing brought my thoughts back to the present. Familiar songs rang through that love-filled room, as we were led in worship by Wang Ming-Tao and Debra. 'Amazing grace.' 'What a Friend we have in Jesus.' 'All the way my Saviour leads me' – Wang's favourite hymn. Music seemed to swell from the hearts of these people and rise towards heaven. Time flew by. Before I realized it, four and a half hours had passed.

Ping's mother had been hard at work throughout our long visit, preparing food for us all. Our generous hosts had very little of their own, yet they sat us down at a banqueting table. Along came seven courses of excellent Chinese cuisine. How sacrificial they were, stretching their own food to share with the rest of us!

How precious an experience it is, I thought as I looked at each of the pleasant faces there, *to be in the company of seven people who have spent time in prison because of their faith. Here we are eating together, and I know this meal is a royal feast compared to anything they ever had in prison. I feel like leaving the table and just letting them enjoy it!*

Yet I have often heard Brother Andrew, Open Doors founder and president, say that our visits to troubled countries bring great encouragement to the persecuted Church. It's not just the Bibles we offer them. Incredible as it seems, our very companionship touches their hearts.

Praying with that cluster of believers was an experience I will never forget. They seemed most at home in the presence of God. Words of praise poured forth from their grateful hearts like fountains of shimmering water sparkling in the sunlight.

Outside, in Shanghai's never-quiet streets, afternoon shadows were stretching themselves across the city. Couple by couple, Lin's visitors excused themselves regretfully and headed for their own simple dwellings, walking carefully and prayerfully in the knowledge that their movements were still under observation by the authorities. We lingered until last, grasping the old man's words, collecting them like priceless jewels in our memories. Would we ever see him again? How could we rush away?

At last he and his wife excused themselves. Into the Chinese sunset they vanished, living symbols of truth and valour. I watched them go, disappearing down the alleyway. My mind raced over the old man's history. He was a unique, matchless hero of the Christian faith. If the Bible had been written today, Wang Ming-Tao would have been in it.

Wang Ming-Tao's name is virtually unrecognized in the mainstream Western world. His story is rarely repeated. His message is infrequently presented. The circumstances under which he suffered are unfamiliar to most people in North America and Western Europe.

Yet I found great truth to learn from Wang Ming-Tao. And truth remains truth in any part of the globe. While sitting with Wang Ming-Tao I received riches at his hand which I longed to see passed on to brothers and sisters throughout the world.

His painful pilgrimage began with the provincial, isolationist dawning of the Chinese twentieth century. Eighty-plus years brought him into a generation of jet travel and computers. Today he finds himself in a China that is hesitantly making overtures of friendship towards the West.

Who is this man? What does he represent?

How can his message apply to you and to me?

Section II

His Story

'I am Peter . . . I am Peter.'
Wang Ming–Tao

2. The Birth of a Century

The year was 1900. The streets of Peking were in chaos. A terrified group huddled inside the Legation quarter and clung to each other, shuddering at the gunfire that grew closer and closer. Outside the area's protective walls, screams could be heard, and the angry shouts of soldiers.

Over the course of the past fifty years, two wars had set China against Britain and France. Now the Boxer Rebellion was bringing further suffering and sorrow. Years later, Wang Ming-Tao would describe the civil uprising in his autobiography, *A Stone Made Smooth*.[1]

'The Empress Dowager accepted the reports of foolish officials and encouraged the so-called Boxers by offering them rewards to kill all foreigners and Christians. This led to catastrophe and the allied armies entered Peking . . .'

One late June afternoon a young man, quaking with fright, ascended a rickety ladder to look over the wall of the Legation quarter. He could no longer bear the suspense – he could only trust his eyes to reveal the truth. Pulling himself up to gaze into his hometown's familiar streets, he felt sweat chill his face and hands.

Attacking soldiers were right outside the walls!

He went back down the ladder with the fear of death burning in his young heart. He caught sight of his sweet-faced, pregnant wife and their little girl. *Dying is bad enough. But they'll torture us once they get in here. I can't bear to see it . . .*

An insane panic gripped the entire area. More than one suicide occurred that night. The certainty of self-imposed death seemed far less terrifying than the unknown agony that seemed so sure to come. Who could bear to watch the women and children die horribly? It was too much to wait and see.

The young man vanished into a private corner and strangled himself. His wife was left with her little girl. Just over a month later, she found herself with an infant son, delivered into the troubled Chinese city of Peking by his grandmother.

'He is Iron . . .' said the older woman, upon declaring the child healthy. 'Wang Ming-zi.' Twenty years later he would choose a new name to reflect a new spiritual birth.

The Boxer Rebellion eventually claimed the lives of 1,900 Protestant Chinese Christians and 30,000 Roman Catholics. Some 188 Protestant missionaries and forty-seven Roman Catholic priests also lost their lives during that time.

Wang's early years were marred by extreme poverty. His mother managed to secure a place of residence for herself and her two little ones. In the early morning before school in Peking's cluttered streets, her small, black-haired son could be found rummaging through rubbish outside the city's more prosperous homes. Everything that would burn was placed in a sieve and carried home for the fire. This would reduce the family's fuel expense so that more food could be bought.

Despite the arduous life that he lived, the little boy was an avid reader. He puzzled over the meaning of words. And as he grew older the meaning of life intrigued him. Rich and poor. Life and death.

'Dead – finished!' So he wrote in his book. 'I could not bring myself to accept its inevitability. I wanted to find a road to life. I cannot recall exactly how old I was when I began to turn these questions over in my mind. I know that it was before I began to go to school and certainly when I was between six and nine.'

The China of Wang Ming-Tao's childhood was an embattled nation. In the past two hundred years, centuries of fine culture and advanced civilization had been intruded upon by Western traders and missionaries. The isolationism that China had long enjoyed had been interrupted. Now she stood snarling in open rebellion against the foreign influences that seemed to have disrupted her glorious independence. To make matters worse, internal conflicts were forever taking their toll in innocent lives.

Against this backdrop, a very observant child was growing up unnoticed in the city then known as Peking. He watched the struggles of the people around him, and considered not only their behaviour, but the values that caused them to conduct themselves in a given manner. The boy saw his mother work far too hard in order to make up for the losses she suffered at the hands of the unscrupulous.

Why was Life so bad? Was Death the only alternative?

A brilliant mind explored those mysteries again and again, investigating them from every possible angle. 'I feared death but knew that sooner or later I could not escape from it. I sought long life but had no means of ensuring it. I was pessimistic; I lost hope. No one could comfort me or bring me happiness. Whatever I gave myself to study or spent time in recreation my spirits would rise, but whenever I thought of human mortality I became conscious of bitter pain.'

But at last a schoolmate approached him and began to speak to him about a personal relationship with Deity. He was a kind-faced boy, a friend in whom Wang had often seen strength of character and a loving attitude.

'I want to talk to you about God . . .' the young man spoke softly to his friend one afternoon in Wang's fourteenth year.

In that pivotal conversation he explained the singular plan of spiritual salvation begun on a faraway Jerusalem cross nearly two thousand years before. Slowly, slowly, the answers to the puzzled boy's questions began to emerge in his mind. Yes, there was life after death – eternal life made possible by the sacrifice of Jesus Christ's life. God had chosen to die for men.

And yes, there was hope for the sinsickness that seemed to poison the lives of so many. People could be changed. They could be transformed by the renewing of their minds.

'I was clearly aware of the change that had taken place in me but I did not understand what it was all about. Previously I had given expression to all sorts of bad language and engaged in all sorts of evil conduct without any sorrow or any sense of shame whatever. But after that year I was completely different . . . From one point of view I now had faith, I had purpose, and I had the will to climb higher. I had no wish to pass my days stupidly and worthlessly . . . but from another point of view there was still conflict within my heart, and I felt the opposing influences of good and evil.'

Young Wang was never able to take lightly the vast questions of the universe. He was a deep-thinking lad, a person of unusual seriousness. His inner depths were forever being plumbed by his own perfectionism and desire for integrity. Like Paul he wrestled with the dilemma of 'the good that I wish, I do not do; but I practice the very evil that I do not wish . . .' (Rom. 7.15 NAS).

Yet, despite his frustrations and setbacks, his spiritual growth continued. As the twentieth-century history of China exploded around him like breakers in a turbulent sea, he drew closer and closer to the Prince of Peace, to the inner calm that only God could give.

Having seen the disorder that diplomatic miscalculations could bring, Wang had often thought that perhaps a political future would be his calling. But at fifteen, he and the young man who had led him to God walked thoughtfully along a Peking street.

Their conversation had been somewhat superficial, but all at once Wang's friend asked, 'Have you made up your mind what you should do in the future?'

'I've never thought about it. I suppose I'll do whatever I want.'

'That,' he told him, 'will never do. You must have a purpose. You'd better make up your mind.'

The boy admired his friend, and respected his opinion. But a struggle began that lasted for five long years. God was clearly calling Wang into His service. And Wang was not quite ready to make such a permanent commitment.

Finally, at twenty, after a great battle with physical illness and spiritual uncertainty, the decision was made.

'By the spring of 1920 I had unconditionally submitted to God and was now willing to respond to His call . . .'

The choice was finally clear. Service to God was the future of the man. The outward course would be set by the Creator. And soon another event occurred which would forever change his inward direction.

A new student arrived at Wang's school. In the context of a conversation he asked an age-old question: 'What about the sin in our lives?'

Wang raged inside. *How could any sin remain in a good Christian like me?* he thought to himself as he tried to respond coolly to the inquisitive student.

'Some believers are very enthusiastic and they work industriously. However, they do this not to glorify God but to glorify themselves,' the schoolmate continued.

Wang was extremely irritated by the words. But deep within his ever-introspective heart, he knew the truth. He was annoyed. And he was annoyed for one simple reason – he was guilty. Up until that night he had considered himself superior to other believers, whether leaders, elders or pastors. His ideals seemed far beyond those of the people he observed around him.

'But that evening,' he reported years later, 'when I knelt by my bed to confess my sins, everything was changed. Everybody else faded out and I was left alone with God. I became conscious of the depravity within me . . . In the presence of God I feared and trembled. The more I prayed, the more conscious I became of my unworthiness. I was unclean, vicious and hateful.

'I uttered no sound as I knelt by my bed, but I was humbled to the dust . . . I realized that were it not for the blood of Christ I would have no hope whatever of entering the presence of God.

'I dedicated myself anew to Him. I was willing to obey Him fully. I was ready to serve Him faithfully all my life. And from that day on my life was gradually but wonderfully changed!'

From that day forth he would be known as Wang Ming-Tao – 'revealing or understanding the Word'. His beginnings could hardly have been less impressive.

But over the course of the next sixty-plus years the remarkable life of Wang Ming-Tao would forever change the course of the Chinese Christian Church.

Note

1. Wang Ming-Tao, *A Stone Made Smooth*, (Mayflower Christian Books, Hants 1981).

3. Unpopular Pathways

A winter wind howled across the Chinese landscape. Each tree, every shrub and plant was rigid, stiffened by weeks of unrelenting frost. As the little group of men made their way along a lonely riverside, the ground was covered with several inches of snow, the river hidden beneath heavy layers of ice.

At last they stopped. A small bridge crossed the river, and beneath it a cascade continued to flow, its activity unhindered by ice. The men stood staring at the little waterfall and the unfrozen pool that surrounded it. They began to take off the warm coats and clothing they wore.

Quickly, trembling with cold, they slipped into thin garments. One of them suddenly stepped into the icy river waters, and another followed.

As Wang Ming-Tao stepped into the water, he closed his eyes and uttered a silent prayer. *Lord, you know what this will cost me. And you know I'm doing it because I want to obey you. Please bless me Heavenly Father.*

They gently lowered Wang into the icy stream. He placed one hand upon his companions' clasped fingers, and the other behind his back. He spoke softly, and reverently. 'In the name of the Father and the Son and the Holy Spirit . . .'

As Wang re-emerged his long hair froze immediately. His thin clothing stiffed against his young body. He was chilled to the bone. He was about to lose his job because of this experience. But he was obedient. And that was all that mattered to him. Five other students followed him into the icy water baptism that day.

Wang's decision to experience baptism by immersion was not taken lightly. He had been comfortably employed as a teacher in a Presbyterian school. When he informed his supervisors of his intention regarding baptism, they simply said, 'If you are immersed, you will have to leave the school. And if any students follow your example, they'll have to leave, too.'

He later described the dilemma. 'So two possible paths lay before me. One path was to go ahead and to be baptized by immersion. But what would this involve? I faced at least three difficulties. First, I would immediately lose my occupation. Second, my reputation would suffer. Up to that time I had been very concerned about 'face', and I had enjoyed fame . . . Third, my future plans would come to nothing . . .'

One night Wang's principal came to his room. 'What have you decided to do about the baptism issue?'

Wang studied the older man carefully. No doubt the three 'difficulties' passed through his mind at that moment. But he replied, 'I'm going to be baptized by immersion, sir. I believe it's what God would have me do.'

The principal handed the young man a bag of coins to cover his fare to Peking. 'I want you to leave school tonight.'

'There's no train tonight, sir. The last train has already gone. And even if I were to stay in an inn I'd need a little while to collect my things and to hand over my responsibilities.'

Reluctantly the principal allowed him to stay until morning. Wang Ming-Tao had disrupted his life by making his first strong stance against the religious establishment. It would not be his last.

Wang decision caused him more grief than one could have imagined possible. Nearly everyone he knew turned against him. 'Being surrounded by hostility was indeed an unpleasant experience. I felt that if only I could find a job I would lessen the grief at home and reduce misunderstandings among my acquaintances . . . During that period I was reluctant to go outside the front gate of our courtyard, because as soon as I got outside I would meet people with whom I was acquainted and some whom I found it difficult to see.'

The crisis of that time led Wang Ming-Tao to a Scripture that deeply touched him. 'There hath no temptation taken you but such as is common to man: but God is faithful who will not suffer you to be tempted above that ye are able; but will with the temptation also make a way to escape, that ye may be able to bear it' (1 Cor. 10. 13 KJV).

The Word of God had always been of great importance to the young man. But now he began to search the Scriptures more fully than ever. He devoured all he read. His keen mind and education made it possible for him to grasp the deeper meanings of the Bible.

His understanding of God's Word to man led him to teaching opportunities. He began to share with others, and before long, Bible studies were springing up all around him. He preached an uncompromising Gospel, based on diligent conformance to the character and attitudes of Jesus Christ.

His unwavering desire for purity among God's people caused him to be criticized. He was labelled 'proud', 'judgmental', 'unforgiving'. And yet his ministry grew. His love for God and his evident sincerity and faithfulness drew hungry Christians into his meetings, seeking growth and encouragement in their own pilgrim walk.

Wang Ming-Tao was wounded by the disapproval of those around him. He was a sensitive man, and as always deeply thoughtful. 'During that period I had to taste the flavour of unlimited misfortunes and to eat all kinds of bitterness . . . Derision, misunderstanding, scoffing, persecution, grief – I have tasted them again and again . . . "We went through fire and through water;

but thou broughtest us out into a wealthy place" (Ps. 66. 12 KJV). Previously I had only read the words of this Psalm. But now I have experienced them.'

As his ministry grew more and more successful, Wang heard a whispered message from time to time, creeping into his thoughts and causing him to wonder if he should take a different course. By the early 1930s he had preached to tens of thousands of people. He was making evangelistic journeys, and his name was becoming recognized throughout China.

Perhaps, he thought to himself as he rattle across the Chinese countryside in rickety train, *I should ease up a bit in my point of view. Suppose I remove from my preaching all those passages that give offense . . . Suppose I cease to teach the kind of doctrines some people think of as myths . . . Suppose I no longer censure apostasy . . .*

I could win greater honour . . . I could avoid being misunderstood . . . I could become an influential and honourable personality in the church.

With the gentleness only a Heavenly Father can have for His beloved children, a still, small voice corrected Pastor Wang. He began to recognize the fact that no one but the enemy of God's Holy Scripture would inspire him to such thoughts. And, once again, Wang Ming-Tao made a decision. He took 'the road less travelled by . . .' And in doing so he was blessed by the Master whom he served.

By the spring of 1933 so many people were attending Wang's Peking worship service that it became necessary for him to rent a large hall in the city. It could accommodate 200 people comfortably, but before long the number had grown to 450. Another larger building was acquired. Soon this was also too small.

At last it was clear that a structure needed to be built. Designs were submitted. Building began. On 7 July, 1937, the 'Marco Polo Bridge Incident' heralded the outbreak of fighting between Japan and China. On 1 August 'The Christians' Tabernacle' was dedicated. The Japanese army entered Peking on 8 August.

Although the Japanese occupation limited Wang Ming-Tao's freedom, the work continued. The meeting hall was a great blessing to his congregation. It provided protection from the summer's blazing heat. And when winter came, the wind was turned away by the sturdy walls. 'The Christians' Tabernacle' was Wang Ming-Tao's visible assurance that God was blessing his ministry.

During this time his sermons were being printed and distributed throughout China. He was respected and revered despite the criticism that haunted him. And his position regarding his own church was well-publicized everywhere.

Wang Ming-Tao wanted his church to be independent. His opinion was that it should be self-supporting, not requiring financial aid from outside China. He also believed that it should be self-governed, without input from anyone but its own fellowship of Chinese believers. And he was of the mind that those who taught and preached within the church should be Chinese, individuals who could understand the needs and circumstances of those to whom they spoke.

Wang's church thrived for many years. His reputation grew and flourished. And as time passed, the political circumstances within China were being gradually transformed. By the time the Sino-Japanese war was concluded in 1945, a more sinister conflict had begun.

The Nationalists, led by the forces of Chiang Kai-Shek, were soon at war with Mao Tse-Tung's Marxist troops. The travail continued for four years. Eventually the Nationalist troops were defeated, and most of the Chinese people welcomed Mao. He communicated his dream of a new China in terms that inspired people to look forward to better days.

But his plan for the future was not to be accomplished without bloodshed. As David H. Adeney reports in *China, The Church's Long March* [1], 'Mao's vision was to create not only a new society but a new kind of person. Millions were killed, and many others fled with the Nationalists to Taiwan.'

During this time the persecution of Christians became widespread throughout China. Just before the Communist government came into power in 1949, Wang Ming-Tao had refused to sign a document demanding his loyalty to the Communist Party. It stated that the Christian Church in China was a tool of imperialism.

Subsequent to his manifesto, the Three-Self Patriotic Movement was introduced. The Church in China, said the new Communist government, was to be self-governing, self-supporting and self-propagating. Wang had long clung to those very principles himself, in the operation of his own church. But the difference lay in the purpose. The Communists were setting up their own form of 'Christianity' in order to control the Christian Church.

Wang Ming-Tao immediately saw through the facade. And although the ideals of the Three-Self were very compatible with his philosophy, he refused to have any part of the system. Instead of co-operating, Wang did exactly what he had done so many times in the past: he stood up and denounced that of which he disapproved.

In the introduction to *A Call to the Church* [2], a compilation of Wang's messages, the results of his denouncement are reported: 'On August 7, 1955, after midnight, Pastor and Mrs Wang, with a number of Christians from The Tabernacle, were arrested, bound and taken to jail. Wang was given a fifteen-year sentence on the grounds that he was a counter-revolutionary. Within a few weeks his church closed down.'

But for Wang, that imprisonment was only the beginning of sorrows. Some thirty years later he told me, 'Living in this world, a person will encounter three strong temptations. The first is the temptation of material things. The second temptation is that of vanity. The third temptation is of the flesh. I have encountered all of these . . . and thanks be to God, for none of these things did I ever fall.

'But at the end I fell, but for what reasons? Fear.

'Only after I fell did I understand what it says in Proverbs 29:25 KJV: "The fear of man bringeth a snare: but whoso putteth his trust in the Lord shall be safe." I did not fall on account of money nor on account of vain glory nor even for the lust of the flesh. I fell because of fear.

'And now, after many years of great trial, I have learned another lesson. Even fear will give way to victory!'

Notes

1. Adeney, David H., *China, The Church's Long March* (Regal Books, Ventura, CA. 1985), p.44.
2. Wang Ming-Tao, *A Call to the Church* (Christian Literature Crusade, Fort Washington, PA. 1983), p.9.

4. Despair, Denial and Defiance

His heart thundering inside his chest, the slender fifty-five-year-old man was roughly shoved into the cell. He caught his balance shakily as he heard the door lock solidly behind him. Somewhat dazed, he tried to absorb the reality of the situation. The two prisoners who already inhabited the small, fetid cubicle stared at him icily.

Wang Ming-Tao had been sentenced under Category Three of China's penal code: death row. He was considered a counter-revolutionary by the Communist government, and if the rumours he had heard about imprisoned Christians were even partially true, he had some terrifying days ahead.

The first man smirked haughtily at the new inmate's evident terror. 'Do you know what they're going to do to you?'

Wang shook his head mutely.

'First they're going to lay you down on the floor . . .'

Wang's two cellmates eyed each other knowingly.

'Then they'll stick a gun at your head and pull the trigger.'

A strange sense of relief flooded Wang at the thought of sudden, final death. It would be better than a lifetime in this foul-smelling, horror-filled place. But the story continued.

'They know how to shoot people like you, preacher. The bullet won't go through your brain. They'll put it through your head so it goes in one side and out the other. The pain is what kills you, man. The pain . . .' he paused meaningfully, 'and the slow, slow bleeding.'

The two men began to laugh uproariously. Wang Ming-Tao had never considered himself a courageous man. He was firm in his convictions, yes. And he had a will of iron when it came to holding his position in debate. But as for pain? The thought of it made his limbs weak. He was fully unprepared for the kind of hideous mistreatment that made these prisons infamous.

Wang Ming-Tao prayed in his spirit as the days crawled by. 'Oh God, I don't deny your existence, but I don't want to serve you any more!' He whispered the words sadly to heaven. 'No matter how I pray to you, nothing changes.'

The two men with whom he shared his pitiful quarters were Mo and Huang. Neither of them was a Christian believer. Although prisoners themselves, they seemed bent on seeing Wang change his mind. If he did, they might even have hoped that their own terms might be shortened as a reward.

In the waning hours of 1955, one of them said, 'This is the dawn of a new year. Let's talk about our thoughts.'

Wang shared his turmoil with the men. He expressed the fact that he was beginning to doubt the existence of God. His cellmates seemed pleased. 'Good! We want to congratulate you. You'll soon be released from jail.'

The other chuckled. 'You know, of course, that Communists don't believe in God. Now that you've got your own doubts, you can get out of here. You ought to start writing your appeal today!'

Thoughtfully, regretfully, Wang Ming-Tao began to write. During that time, there had been no court hearing for more than a month. Every day ended as it began, with Wang simply locked inside the jail with his two cellmates.

'Hurry! Finish it today . . . it's New Year, and you'll start 1956 off right.'

Once Wang's appeal was in the hands of the Communist authorities, a hearing was quickly scheduled. Standing before his accusers, the weary man admitted, 'Yes . . . I suppose I have begun to doubt the existence of God . . .'

Now, instead of being handled roughly, Wang found himself being treated very kindly. Very kindly indeed. He was invited to sit beside a warm stove with one of the local Communist leaders, who was a prison judge.

'I have read your report and I'm very happy. As last you have doubts about God. You know, Communists very much welcome Christians who have such doubts.'

The two men looked at each other silently, trying to determine what the other was thinking. The prison judge spoke again. 'I've had differing ideas with regard to you. First I was thinking of killing you. But then I saw your talent and I thought of keeping you to work for the government.'

Wang was somewhat perplexed. 'What kind of work could I do for the government?'

'The same work you've always done, Wang. You can preach!'

The prison judge laughed. 'You can still do it. You just speak with authority and pretend. It doesn't matter what's inside your heart. Your mouth can still get the job done.'

Wang was deeply distressed by these words. Since his Christian conversion at fourteen years of age, he had chosen not to speak a word of untruth. For forty-one long years he had hated lies. And now that was the very thing he was expected to do.

After much soul-searching, Wang Ming-Tao refused the offer of release. He might not be sure about God, but he was still quite certain that he could not live a hypocritical life.

His cellmates scoffed him. 'You're crazy. There's nothing to it. You just keep lying. Eventually you won't think anything of it – you'll get used to it!'

Nevertheless Wang stood firm in his resolve, until he heard that his beloved wife was in grave danger. He received word that Debra was not eating properly. It was reported to him that she was growing critically weak because of the unnourishing food she was receiving in prison. She would not survive if something were not done.

After this distressing news reached him, Wang wrote the lie that eventually led to his release from prison. 'I'm willing to accept the offer. I will preach the Word the way he wants me to.' Wang never meant to do so, but by now he was willing to pretend.

Within two months, the prison judge said, 'You and your wife are good prisoners. The government would like to be lenient with you.'

Soon Wang's lies were compounded. 'Yes, I'll join the Three-Self church when I'm released.' He had no intention of doing such a thing. But he was afraid he would never be released unless he said he would.

Wang could not have been more miserable. For years he had specifically preached against dishonesty. How could it be that he had chosen to become a liar himself just to obtain his release from prison?

Heartsick and guilty, he sat in the corner of his reeking cell, self-destructive thoughts clouding his mind in darkness. *I'll get my wife out of prison. I'll get her to her mother's place where she'll be safe. Then I'll jump from some high place and kill myself. There is no reason for me to live. After this, how can I go on?*

After his release, Wang was asked to develop a written report. No matter what the authorities told him to say, he wrote it down. He wrote from nine in the evening until twelve noon. The next day when he was asked to change the wording, change it he did.

The next humiliation came when he was forced to take his report to the Youth League.

'But . . . I've never approved of the Youth League,' Wang weakly responded.

'Sorry. That's where you'll have to read it. If you don't, your wife won't be released.'

Wang stood before the Youth League and recited his report – all lies from beginning to end. His head was hung low, his eyes downcast.

Following his unhappy recital, a young man asked for a copy of the statement Wang had made. Shortly afterwards, the entire text appeared in the popular Three-Self Patriotic Movement (TSPM) *Tien Feng Magazine*. Wang Ming-Tao was sick at heart. Soon his body became ill, too.

It was widely reported that he wandered the streets of the city near his home murmuring, 'I am Peter . . . I am Peter.'

For months, the government waited for him to begin preaching. The Three-Self church waited for him to join. At last they realized that he had no intention of keeping the 'word' he had given in his false report. Wang and his wife were re-arrested. And this time a more severe order came down.

Wang Ming-Tao had clearly determined not to change his 'counter-revolutionary' attitude. He was therefore sentenced to life imprisonment, and stripped of his political rights. His wife Liu Qing Wun – Debra – was sentenced to fifteen years' imprisonment.

Wang Ming-Tao had come to the end. He lost hope completely. Grieving and in despair, there was no place to hide from himself. He had lied. He had stumbled. He had no place on earth to go for solace. All that lay ahead of him was death. For days he stared sullenly at the dreary place in which he was forever to remain. No future. No tomorrow. Nothing for which to live.

But one day, whether morning or night he could never say, a Scripture floated through his agonized spirit – a verse he had memorized at the age of twenty-one.

'But as for me, I keep watch for the Lord, I wait in hope for God my Saviour; my God will hear me. Do not gloat over me, my enemy! Though I have fallen, I will rise. Though I sit in darkness, the Lord will be my light. Because I have sinned against him, I will bear the Lord's wrath, until he pleads my case and establishes my right. He will bring me out into the light; I will see his justice' (Micah 7:7–9 NIV).

Slowly, slowly the realization dawned. Wang Ming-Tao understood that he was sentenced to life imprisonment because he had sinned against his God. And what kind of sin had he committed? He had lied! *For somebody else to lie is one thing,* he quietly told himself. *But for Wang Ming-Tao to lie is his greatest sin. Why? Because I've hated lying so much for so long. I, of all people, should have been prepared for such a test. And yet I failed. I have no reason to be angry with God. I have brought this all upon myself!*

Within a few days, Wang was assigned to the prison clinic. Although most of the people there were quite ill, there was sunlight. There was relief from the dank filth. It was definitely an improvement over the vile place he had inhabited before.

In Wang Ming-Tao's first report he had written nothing but untruths. Fear had moved his pen for him, causing him to record things that were in no way honest or genuine. But by now he had nothing to fear. Nothing at all.

'I have never violated any law!' he boldly wrote. 'I was imprisoned simply because I stood firm against the Three-Self movement. I will still stand against them . . .'

Wang Ming-Tao wrote and wrote. He wrote for ten solid months. He filled almost a thousand sheets of paper. He wrote carefully, utilizing the smallest characters possible. His defiant report struck nerves in all who read it. It irritated some, and enraged others. The battle with Wang Ming-Tao had taken a strange new twist.

Wang Ming-Tao was no longer afraid!

5. The Key to the Prison.

Against the silver-grey sky, hundreds of crimson flags fluttered atop the majestic buildings that line Chang-An Avenue. Peking's proudest display of Communist authority reigned in undisputed power over the late afternoon, proclaiming China's strength and glory to all who gazed upon the scene. Over looking it all stood the portrait of Mao Tse-Tung.

Not many miles away, however, within the confines of a prison, a far different picture of Communist activity was being painted. Outside the building, the pitiful cries were muffled. The merciless blows falling against already bruised flesh could not be heard at all. But on that day, as upon every other, Christian believers were being 'encouraged' to change their way of thinking. And they paid for their uncomprising faith in blood and breathtaking pain.

The stories are rarely told to the Western visitor. Chinese Christians would rather smile and praise God than recall the suffering that was inflicted upon them during their incarceration. Stories have to be carefully drawn from reluctant souls with shining eyes who have clearly 'forgiven those who have trespassed against them'.

And yet some tales have been repeated enough by reliable sources to be known facts.

There was the medical doctor who refused to confess that Chairman Mao was bigger than his Christ. He was stripped naked, beaten and humiliated. At last he was hanged for his faith.

There was the woman who awoke from a beating that had rendered her unconscious, finding herself lying in urine and faecal matter, covered with vermin. After asking her Lord for strength and wisdom, she begged Him to allow her to spread the Gospel in that hideous place.

Suddenly the idea struck her that she might clean up the filthy cells. She volunteered. As she scrubbed and scoured, her witness to her fellow inmates led dozens to Jesus Christ.

There was the lonely, heartbroken schoolteacher who bravely began to sing the lovely old hymn, 'All the way my Saviour leads me', in the prison courtyard. One by one, other Christians began to find hope in the gently sung words. They began to share their belief in Jesus with others. Within days, the Gospel had been accepted by dozens of non-Christian prisoners.

The Chinese prison is a place best forgotten by those who have been fortunate enough to be released from it with their lives. Its reputation for cruelty, inhumane conditions and mental torture is a tribute to the unending bent towards cruelty exhibited by some of the Communist authorities who operate it.

And yet the lessons of the place are not meant to be removed from the memory. The saints that emerge from its horrors have faces that gleam like the morning sun. Their spirits have been set free from the yoke of worldliness. Their hearts are untouched by fear. They have lost everything. And they have gained heaven.

By the end of the 1970s, Wang Ming-Tao had resigned himself to the fact that he would die in prison. And he was content with that understanding – nothing could threaten the man by that time. Everything that could possibly be done to him had been done. And still he lived.

One afternoon his son appeared at the prison to take him home. 'What are you doing here? Why have you come?' The now-old man could not grasp the meaning of his son's unexpected appearance.

'I just received this message: "Upon receipt come quickly to fetch home Wang Ming-Tao." Didn't you send it?'

Wang's son had assumed the message had come from his father. But that was not the case. The prison authorities wanted to be rid of the steely preacher and they had summoned his son.

'I will not go!' announced Wang. He was determined to remain until his case was entirely cleared up. 'I was imprisoned on account of my faith and not because I committed any crime. I thank God that from the time of my conversion right up until my imprisonment there was nothing that I needed to be ashamed of. Until it's clear that I am in prison solely because of my faith I will not go!'

'But Father, things are terrible here. If you leave you'll be at liberty . . .'

'I don't care. My case must be settled with absolute clarity. Then I can walk out of the prison gate with my head held high and my arms swinging.'

And so it was that in 1980, frail, nearly blind and all-but-deaf, at eighty years of age this old shepherd Wang Ming-Tao was finally released from prison. His beloved wife had been sent home three years before for health reasons. Their son was able to find a home for them in Shanghai. And it was in that great city that I met them for the first time in Lin's warm, friendly apartment.

One day, after our first encounter, I was able to talk to Wang Ming-Tao about his prison experience. I remember sitting in his own home, and wondering how I could have stood prison life. There was so much to learn from these ones whose lives had been tested so severely. Theirs was a holiness I knew I wanted. But how had they walked the pilgrimage that had brought them to such a holy lifestyle?

'Uncle, did you face many temptations in prisons?' I began.

'You'd be surprised at what tempts a person. Inside prison I met a man from Poland. He had been sentenced because of some financial reasons. Every month this man received a big paper box of food – cookies, cheese and soft drinks. He never counted his cookies! One day he was sent to labour camp and I was left alone with all the food.

'He had so much and I knew he'd never miss any of it. I really was tempted to steal a morsel or two – very tempted. But I knew if I did and an official saw me, the word would be spread that Wang Ming-Tao stole food . . . and that would bring dishonour to our Lord.'

Oh my word, I found myself thinking. *This man measures holiness right down to the last cookie crumb*! I had a growing feeling that his burning desire for God's glory might be the secret, the key to the depth of the walk he had found with the Lord. How much I wanted to learn from this man. I studied that time-etched face which told so powerful a story. Many of his teeth were gone. He was nearly blind. Yet such a beauty was present in his joyful smile, a beauty born of a life lived in the presence of his Lord.

'Were there other temptations?' I urged.

He nodded. 'Physical torture causes you to . . .'

'Stop!' His wife suddenly interrupted. 'There are many things you should not talk about!'

He looked at her lovingly, and relaxed a bit. There was a quiet moment and I knew the subject should be changed. Certainly, I did not want this faithful servant of God to speak on any topic that could cause him trouble. I sought only that secret which had fuelled this man's burning desire for the beauty of God. Was it the life of prayer or of praise in prison? 'Did you pray every day inside the prison?' I asked.

'In prison, you cannot pray aloud and you cannot close your eyes when you pray. You just have to pray silently in your heart.'

'How about singing hymns?'

'Before I came out from prison, in the later years, I would always sing hymns in the courtyard. Prisoners would ask, "What are you singing?" The officers knew, but they couldn't control me. They knew that Wang Ming-Tao could no longer be re-educated. They gave up.'

His wife laughed, and shook her head. 'I think the people in charge of the prison gave him special treatment. Nobody is allowed to hum any song inside prison. Nobody is allowed to talk or discuss anything. But Wang Ming-Tao could roam around and sing every day in the courtyard!' She laughed again and I joined her. I could well imagine this child of God delighting in the praise of his Father, despite every pull to the contrary.

The old man smile. 'One time an officer said to me, "You are improving now. You don't spread the Gospel anymore."

'I said, "It's not that I don't want to spread the Gospel. It's just that nobody would want to listen." If people are put in here because of their faith, who would want to hear about a faith that gets you into that kind of trouble?'

Wang's wife gently hushed him from further description, ever-vigilant of his outspoken ways. She turned to me: 'Please, just share what he has said about God's Word. That is all that is important.'

Watching the two together, I was touched by her care. *How she loves him*, I thought myself. *They were separated from each other for almost twenty-three years. And look at the commitment they have to each other. They're still very much in love! It's a beautiful thing to behold.*

'Just share what he's said about the Lord's Word . . .' This utter dependence upon the Word of God must have been a big part of the secret to this couple's victory in suffering. Not only in prison did they draw so heavily upon God's Word, but here in their home as well where the walls are decorated with Scriptures in graceful Chinese characters. One passage seemed particularly right to describe the life of Wang Ming-Tao.

'Uncle, there's a Bible passage that speaks to me of you,' I said.

He listened carefully as I began. '"We do not want you to be uninformed, brothers, about the hardships we suffered in the province of Asia. We were under great pressure, far beyond our ability to endure, so that we despaired even of life. Indeed, in our hearts we felt the sentence of death. But this happened that we might not rely on ourselves but on God, who raises the dead" (2 Cor. 1.8, 9 NIV).

'You have known moments of such deep cost. And you have learned deep reliance upon God in that place of pain. How did God meet you in your greatest need and bring His victory?'

The old man paused for only a moment. 'When in desperation, I remembered the Bible and the Word of God gave me strength. One particular day I suddenly remembered Isaiah 55: "You will go out in joy and be led forth in peace; the mountains and hills will burst into song before you, and all the trees of the field will clap their hands. Instead of the thornbush will grow the pine tree, and instead of briers the myrtle will grow. This will be for the Lord's renown, for an everlasting sign, which will not be destroyed"' (Isa. 55.12, 13 NIV).

Joy glimmering in his wise old eyes, Wang continued, 'It is true! After a few years, I came out of prison. Before I recalled those verses, I believed that I would stay in prison for ever. I really thought I would die there. But the Word said, "You will come out with joy". God's word is very wonderful. If you memorize it well – the promises and lessons – then in times of need it will bring you strength, comfort and hope.'

The Word of God, then. By filling his mind and soul with it, this old saint had found victory. The same seemed true of prayer.

He continued, 'The Bible says "pray without ceasing". There is no limit to prayer. Whenever and wherever you are, in a car, on the street, you can always pray. If you are on a bike, you can't close your eyes, but you can certainly pray silently in you heart.

'Inside prison, I could not close my eyes and pray. But every time I sat around people who were conversing, I'd still pray in my heart. At night while lying down in bed I would pray. There is no limit, no formality – kneel down, stand up, lie down, sit down, anywhere, any time you can pray.

'Keep praying, keep asking!'

'Is this, then, what you would say to me and to my brothers and my sisters in the West who long for the comfort and victory of God in their struggles? We are hungry to know, Uncle.'

'In Bunyan's *Pilgrim's Progress* a Christian and his experiences are described. I have been through similar encounters. When I was locked up, I voiced my complaints and cursed God.

'The Christians in the book did the same when they were desperate. Those who were locked up by the giant were in despair. They were inside a steel gate and they couldn't come out. Later they got a key, opened the steel gate and they were able to leave. What key was that? That key was the Word of God. Through the Word of God they got out from their desperation.

'It is very, very important that you memorize the Bible well. You don't have to remember what book or what verse. Just remember the Word!

'It was the Word of God that gave me the very best moment in my life.'

'The best moment, Uncle? What was that?' *Perhaps the time he left the prison*, I thought. *Or maybe earlier, easier days before imprisonment.*

Not with this man. His desire for holiness gave him a very different perspective.

'The best moment in my life was when I overcame my lies.'

'When you overcame your lies?'

48

'Yes. When that moment came, my heart rejoiced. I recovered joy, peace and strength. Before I confessed my sins, there was a long period of time during which I didn't want to live. If it weren't for God's protection, I would have been dead by now.

'But it was the Word of God that rescued me . . .'

'So is this your answer to those in turmoil, those in conflict, those who are suffering?' I asked. My mind flashed, for a moment, to the many answers our modern world offers us to deal with the stresses and problems of life.

For this pair, whose lives could have been engulfed by suffering, the answer was disarmingly simple.

The old man glanced at his wife and warm smiles of understanding creased both of their faces. There was no other possible response in either of their minds. How can you help those who are suffering?

'Share the Word of God with them!'

Section III

His Ache

'Denial is denial. The truth shall make you free.'

6. Churches in Conflict

One by one they arrive. Dressed unobtrusively in blues, greys and greens, they quietly greet each other and happily settle into the vacant chairs that await them. There is a spirit of anticipation, a mood of excitement in the air. With evident delight they acknowledge the arrival of each new individual and couple. And before long they are singing.

After a time of praise and worship, an older gentleman stands and prays. Each member of the little group passes a small scrap of paper to him. He gathers the carefully printed slips, quickly puts them in order and begins to read. He has in his hands the entire scriptural text for his Bible Study lesson.

The message is followed by a period of heartfelt prayer. It is evident, even to a stranger from across the sea, that these people care greatly for one another. Their intercession for each individual's personal needs is deeply moving. They pray for themselves. For their nation. For the world beyond that sparsely furnished little room.

Hours go quickly by. At last, the little gathering of Christian believers slowly begins to dissolve, each person or pair vanishing into the village as inconspicuously as they appeared. The following week, if the Lord allows, they will all meet again. The Chinese house church meeting has ended.

Today the Christian community in China thrives in just such a setting. It has been well publicized that worship is now legal within the People's Republic of China, that the government has loosened its control in recent years. The government-sponsored Three-Self Patriotic Movement (TSPM) has its own churches, preachers and congregations. Many relieved Christians attend the Three-Self services, thankful to be free to sing, pray and receive some spiritual guidance.

But the pulsebeat of China's invisible Christian body throbs strongly, powerfully in the house churches. Here believers can safely come, able to trust the familiar faces that appear week after week. Here they can be sure that the one who teaches the Word of God lives by that Word himself. They know very well that he risks his life to carry its truth to others.

Wang Ming-Tao was arrested because he refused to join the Three-Self movement. His arrest was based on a list of charges which entailed three basic offences. Wang was not sympathetic towards the government, evidenced by the fact that he spoke out against state policy. He did not align himself with the Three-Self Patriotic Movement. And his preaching was 'extremely independent and with unclear motives . . . the whole Protestant movement is being jeopardized'.

Curiously, when the Three-Self concept was introduced to China in the 1920s, it came through the churches themselves. The intention was to promote the building of a self-supporting Chinese Church so that no aid from Western missions would be needed. Originally, the idea was that a localized Church would grow strong and healthy on its own.

Wang's response to this concept was expressed in a statement he made to the Association for United Advancement of Christianity in North China: 'Realizing that the goal of your association is to assist Western-mission-supported churches to become self-dependent, self-supporting and self-propagating, I believe there is no need for me to join. My church has been self-dependent, self-supporting and self-propagating ever since it was established!'

Some years later, when the Three-Self (TSPM) was reintroduced in the 1950s, its meaning had completely changed. When the Three-Self Patriotic Church was formed, it was obvious that its function was to bring the Church under the control of the government. It was a means of diverting Church efforts into a force that would co-operate with and submit to state policy. The key words were Self-Govern: the Church would depart from the governing of imperialism; Self-Support: the Church would reject the financial support of imperialism; Self-Propagate: the Church would not propagate imperialistic ideology, but would proclaim the Gospel of the Chinese Church.

This new movement was hopelessly hooked into politics. Unlike the mission strategy of the 1920s, this was a tool of the Communists, far removed from Wang Ming-Tao's personal principles.

'We must obey God rather than men!' (Acts 5.29 NIV). How many times had Wang preached those words? Now their true meaning was about to be tested like gold in Wang Ming-Tao's heart. He was a man of strong character. He would not compromise easily. When faced with the choice between truth and politics, he chose truth. And in doing so, of course, he chose prison.

'Three-Self has adopted liberal theology,' he would explain to any who would listen. 'And I give you five reasons why liberalism is wrong. Liberals deny the inerrancy of the Bible. The virgin birth of Jesus. The redemption from sin through salvation. The resurrection of the body. The second coming of Jesus. You lose those doctrines and you've lost everything!'

Wang Ming-Tao also felt that believers should not be unequally yoked with non-Christians. There was really no common ground for the two to form a union. How could he join the Three-Self?

Today the Three-Self churches continue throughout the People's Republic of China. And, as always, debate goes on regarding their place in Christendom.

The Chinese Communist Party defines its own view of state religious organizations (quoted from *China, The Church's Long March* by David H. Adeney):

> The basic task of the patriotic religious organizations at all levels is to assist the government in carrying out the policy of freedom of religious beliefs and the personalities of the religious circles continuously to raise their patriotic and socialist awareness . . . all the patriotic religious organizations should obey the leadership of the Party and the government.'[1]

And what does the Party think of religion?

> Religion is an historical phenomenon of a certain stage in the development of human society. It has its stages of growth, development and disappearance . . . In human history religion will ultimately disappear, but it will only naturally disappear after a long period of development of socialism and communism, after all the objective conditions have been fulfilled.[2]

With such a clearly stated view of religion in general and Christianity by inference, a great mistrust is, of course, built into the relationship between the house church movement and the state-sponsored TSPM. To complicate matters further, stories persist within China that seem to reinforce the opinion that certain individuals within the TSPM simply cannot be trusted.

No one would stand more firmly against the official principles of the Three-Self Patriotic Movement than Wang Ming-Tao. He has literally given his life as a statement of disapproval and refusal. But God is a mighty God, and His plans are not thwarted by the political aims of mere men.

Carl Lawrence makes a most interesting observation in his book, *The Church in China, How It Survives and Prospers Under Communism*[3]:

> There are approximately 5,900 registered pastors and preachers in the official TSPM . . . There can be little doubt that many of them are outstanding Christians, who feel that this is a place where the Lord has placed them to minister . . . It is not uncommon to hear a solid evangelical message from the pulpit of the Three-Self churches . . . By allowing these churches to remain open, the government is, in effect, propagating the Gospel of Jesus Christ. The very thing to which they are opposed.

But no wise Chinese is deceived. A clear-eyed realism forces every thinking Christian to know that danger lurks where the Party dwells. And Wang Ming-Tao's unspeakable experiences in prison provide grim warnings: to oppose the state-ordained TSPM is to take one's life in one's hands.

As a whole, Wang's attitude towards the state's TSPM was consistently uncompromising. He vigorously dealt with it according to his faith in God. A man who knew his Bible very well and kept his Christian walk pure since youth, he was able to see the differences between the TSPM and the truth of Jesus Christ.

His 'failure' represents an even more urgent warning. Even the faith of a strong spiritual leader such as Wang Ming-Tao can be shaken under the 're-education' of the Three-Self (TSPM). No Christian should ever underestimate the power of the enemy.

And today, many believers are experiencing the same torment to which Wang was subjected – and they are suffering for precisely the same reason. They have refused to compromise their faith. They have rejected the 'offers' of the Chinese Communist Party. And some have died as martyrs.

Perhaps to the Western Christian these dangers seem remote. The freedom that characterizes Western culture has removed the threat of violence and physical persecution from the minds of many believers in the free world. A certain concern for the persecuted persists in the back of the mind. Yet the strength necessary to cope with beatings, imprisonment and torture remains undeveloped and, seemingly, unnecessary.

But in a chilling statement, Carl Lawrence makes this observation:

> The problem in the West is an erosion of biblical authority leading to the belief that man, not God, is the ultimate authority in the universe. This perversion of essential Christianity is the great problem in the West . . .
>
> Do we all have to undergo the persecution imposed by a Marxism regime? . . .
>
> Persecution comes basically in two forms: physical and mental. Perhaps we are under greater persecution today in the developed countries than we realize.[4]

Mental beating. Spiritual imprisonment. Emotional torture. These are forms of persecution that the Western Christian may well experience when he stands as committed to truth as Wang Ming-Tao. As Lawrence observes, the enemy is not called Marxism. It is called materialism. And every Christian breathing in the Western world has looked that enemy in the eye and either complied with his wishes or rejected his 'offers'.

Some may question whether Wang Ming-Tao has anything to say to the Western world. Is he a sort of Chinese Christian sage whose purity of thought and clarity of concept simply cannot be introduced into our churches?

My own experience, and that of my fellow-workers, is that whenever we visit China we come away with much more than we took in – so great are the spiritual riches we have received from believers like Wang Ming-Tao.

Looking at their example we have come to think about some basic questions. What is it we really face in the West anyway? Is compromise an issue? Is suffering truly a possibility? Is the danger of 'denial' as real to us as it is to a Chinese pastor thousands of miles away who has committed himself to truth?

From him and others who have endured the fire, we have learned much about the spiritual battle facing us all, whatever part of the world we may live in. We have come to realize that if we are unaware of our enemy's identity, we may sell our birthright for a mess of pottage in the form of power. Or prestige. Or popularity. Or prosperity.

But it has also been encouraging to discover that the personal loss, the deep wounds inflicted by words, the unexplainable suffering resulting from sincere Christian efforts may be – just may be – the West's inner counterpart to the East's outward, visible persecution of the believers.

For undoubtedly, our Western Church, too, is in conflict with Satan!

In this sense, then, Wang Ming-Tao's message could not be more important. Is the debate between TSPM and house churches? Or is it between liberal mainstream denominations and local, Bible-believing fellowships? Is the temptation freedom versus imprisonment? Or is it fame and fortune versus anonymous faithfulness?

No matter what the weapon, the pain it inflicts is very real. Conflict is conflict.

No matter what the disguise of the tempter, his intention never changes. Denial is denial.

No matter what the ultimate threat, the defence is always the same. 'Ye shall know the truth, and the truth shall make you free' (John 8.32 KJV).

Denial is denial. The truth shall make you free.

Notes

1. Quoted in Adeney, David H., *China, The Church's Long March* (Regal Books, Ventura, A. 1985), p. 125.
2. Quoted in *China, The Church's Long March,* p. 126.
3. Lawrence, Carl, *The Church in China, How it Survives and Prospers under Communism* (Bethany House Publishers, Minneapolis, MN. 1985), p. 111.
4. *The Church in China. How it Survives and Prospers under Communism.*

His Message – A Living Sermon

'Suffering makes a way for Christians to become holy and perfect.'

Wang Ming-Tao

7. Why Do People Lie?

The subtle secrecy that always accompanied my visits to Wang Ming-Tao was evident again that afternoon. Ever-watchful in their love, those who took me to him communicated caution with their every move. I had asked Stephen Lo and Andy Wee to go ahead of me by several hours. Now two other young men had come to take me to the old man.

Quietly, we made our way towards the familiar doorway. No one wanted to cause Wang difficulties with the Chinese authorities by blatantly bringing Westerners into his home. We all understood the need for discretion.

When the door opened, he caught sight of us and said, 'Praise God! He has sent our brothers from outside to visit us again.'

As his enthusiasm mellowed into a serene smile, he spoke quietly to me. His wife, as always, sat across from him, watching him with love in her eyes and encouragement in her comments. As he had sometimes done before, Wang Ming-Tao preached a private sermon to me that afternoon. And his subject was a familiar one — lying.

'Lying,' he began, 'is not a small thing. Our Lord's Word proves this kind of understanding is wrong. Don't we admit that Jesus is our Lord and our Teacher? We should therefore follow His footsteps. John said, "He committed no sin and no deceit was found in his mouth." He never told a single lie.'

This subject is so close to his heart. I reminded myself of Wang's own spiritual collapse under the assault of the Communists. *He is really speaking from experience.*

And this is what he said:

Why do men tell lies?

We must insistently find out the reasons for lying in this world. We know that God hates lies. And if we are already telling lies, we need to find out why. Perhaps in doing so we can change our evil course.

Some men are *greedy for wealth*. In 2 Kings 5.15–27 NIV, we find the story of Naaman, Elisha and Gehazi. The faithful prophet had rejected the gift offered him by Naaman for is healing. Gehazi, however, had rushed after Naaman and lied in order to acquire for himself a portion of the gift Elisha had rejected.

Gehazi lied because of his greed for wealth. When he saw Naaman place a big load of wealth before the eyes of Elisha, his greedy nature surfaced. Gehazi was hoping that after Elisha accepted the gifts, he would share with him. But Elisha firmly rejected the goods, leaving Gehazi with nothing but disappointment.

When Elisha found out about Gehazi's deception, he confronted his servant. 'Was not my spirit with you when the man got down from his chariot to meet you? Is this the time to take money, or to accept clothes, olive groves, vineyards, flocks, herds, or menservants and maidservants? Naaman's leprosy will cling to you and to your descendants for ever.'

Gehazi lied because of greed. And in the end, he harmed not only himself but his children and descendants. Gehazi didn't just lie once, either. He compounded the problem by lying again and again.

If you don't eliminate greed, you'll never get rid of lies!

Some people lie because they *crave a name*. Ananias and Sapphira depict this problem, as they are described in Acts 5.1–11. They didn't lie because they were greedy like Gehazi. Instead they wanted to make a name for themselves.

Ananias and Sapphira were not punished because they sold their land and kept part of the money. To keep some money is not a sin. Even if they'd kept all the money or hadn't sold their farmland at all – that wouldn't have been a sin either. The property was theirs. And after selling it the money also belonged to them. God would certainly not force them to give.

Peter pointed this out. He said, 'Didn't it belong to you before it was sold? And after it was sold, wasn't the money at your disposal?' If they had honestly given even a little, God would have been pleased.

Their big mistake was privately keeping part of the money and saying that they'd given it all. The sin they committed was 'fraud'. And this kind of fraud didn't cheat man. It defrauded God!

Many Christians are like Ananias and Sapphira. Because they want to have a name, they lie. They really don't have such a big heart but they'd like others to think they do. Their work may not be so good but they'd like other people to say it is. Their lives may not be so devout, but they'd like others to think they are very devoted. They may not really suffer all that much hardship, but they'd like other people to say they are suffering greatly.

These people may exaggerate. Or they may invent from nothing. They may fabricate facts or they may steal the credit from others and put it on themselves.

Wanting a name not only causes lies, it causes one to envy others. It causes people to destroy each other in order to attain the name they want for themselves.

If you don't eliminate the desire for a name, you can never eliminate lies.

Some people lie because they *want power*.

In 2 Samuel 18.9–15, is the story of Absalom. We discover from this text that he not only lied to the people, he also lied to his father King David. And he ended up dead because of it.

Absalom wanted to be king. And in order to win the hearts of his father's subjects, he created a very convincing role for himself. His behaviour amounted to a secret plot. He'd arise early to stand by the side of the road leading into the city gate. There he would talk with the people who had come with complaints to be placed before the king.

If you listen to Absalom's conversation with his father's subjects, he spoke very beautifully and seemed most concerned about them. Whenever anyone approached him, to bow before him, he would reach out his hand, take hold of the person and kiss him. How could a prince be so humble and loving? How could he not touch the hearts of the people?

Within the Church we sometimes find these same sorts of manipulative individuals. They are usually talented and clever. And they soon develop a fictitious reputation for themselves. Their sincerity seems quite genuine for a time. But the more power they attain, the more their thirst for control increases. Eventually, like Absalom, they are destroyed once their motives are no longer able to be kept secret.

Unless you eliminate your desire to have power and control over others, you will never eliminate lies.

There are people who lie because they are *involved in the sin of adultery*.

In 2 Samuel 13 we find the story of Amnon's rape of Tamar. He was smitten with passion for his half-sister. He wanted to possess her. And in order to accomplish his goal, he lied. He created an artificial illness and asked that Tamar be his nurse. Finally, when he was alone with her, he began to force his affections upon her.

Tamar pleaded with him, suggesting that he ask for her hand in marriage. But Amnon would have no delay. He wanted what he wanted. And he wanted it then. He'd gone so far as to lie himself into her presence. He wasn't going to miss his opportunity!

Amnon was killed because of his behaviour. His brother Absalom, no paragon of virtue himself, murdered him to vindicate his sister.

Adultery not only happens by force. It also happens with the co-operation of both parties. And this kind of thing needs to be covered with lies. If a man is unfaithful to his wife, he will eventually have to lie to cover up his misdeeds.

If the two are caught in their affair, they will need to lie even further. Adulterers will lie to explain their behaviour to each other. They will lie to avoid being caught by friends or family. Then, when discovered, they will lie to defend themselves from being harshly judged.

Lying and adultery are inseparably intertwined. We should know this and tremble with fear. If you are unable to escape from your adultery, you will never escape from lies.

There are those who lie *to harm others*.

In 2 Samuel 20 we find the story of Amasa's murder. Joab, David's military chief, had made up his mind to be rid of Amasa. Instead of assaulting him in battle, he greeted the man, threw his arms around him and kissed him. Then he grabbed poor Amasa by the beard and stabbed him with the dagger he had hidden.

How sweet the words! How venomous the plot! How cunning the heart!

Joab was the commander of the Israeli troops. He greeted Amasa, 'How are you, my brother?' Joab seemed really humble and loving to Amasa. Amasa must have thought himself really fortunate to receive so much honour from Joab, and must have been surprised at the unexpected favour.

Why did Joab use this kind of plot? Because he heard that David was going to appoint Amasa as the commander of the army in his place. David was making such a move to protect himself from Absalom, and was looking out for himself as well as for Israel. But Joab wasn't about to let such a thing happen.

So often, when a person would like to harm another, he tells lies. If he does not lie, the other will guard against him and escape from his treacherous hand. A person who would like to harm will not show any feeling or emotion. He holds his bad intentions inside his heart and will not express them.

There are lots and lots of people like Joab. Their hearts are filled with hatred, with envy, with venomous, murderous thoughts. Their words tell of righteousness, love, uprightness and justice. If you just listen to what their mouths say, you can't help but admire and adore them. Sooner or later, however, their actions will give away their true intentions.

If you don't get rid of your desire to harm others, you'll never get rid of lies.

One very common reason for people's lying is *to hide sin*.

In 1 Samuel 15.1–31 we read about King Saul's lies. And in the biblical records of those people who told lies, there is no one who told more lies than Saul. His lies were perfect and considerate, very serious and very horrible. Other people may just lie once or twice at one time. But Saul told five lies simultaneously.

When Saul saw God's prophet, Samuel, he didn't wait for Samuel to open his mouth. He spoke first. Listen to what he said. 'The Lord bless you! I have carried out the Lord's instructions.' This is the first lie.

To this Samuel responded, 'What then is the bleating of sheep in my ears? What is this lowing of cattle that I hear?'

Then Saul told the second lie. 'The soldiers brought them from the Amalekites; they spared the best of the sheep and cattle to sacrifice to the Lord your God . . .'

Afterwards, Saul was scolded by Samuel. He went on to tell his third lie. 'I went on the mission the Lord assigned me. I completely destroyed the Amalekites and brought back Agag their king.'

And then the fourth lie. 'The soldiers took sheep and cattle from the plunder, the best of what was devoted to God.' Later when Saul was insistently questioned by Samuel, he had no way of escaping the facts but honestly confessed because he was trapped. Yet even in the midst of his confession he lied!

'I have sinned. I violated the Lord's command and your instructions. I was afraid of the people and so I gave in to them.' Saul had run out of excuses and had to admit he'd disobeyed. Yet he still lied. He was the king of the whole country, with complete power. All the people were afraid of him. And what did he say? 'I was afraid of the people!'

If a person sins, if he honestly comes before the Lord in repentance and confession God will forgive and consider him as if he'd never sinned. But the Bible warns us, 'He who conceals his sins does not prosper, but whoever confesses and renounces them finds mercy' (Prov. 28.13 NIV).

There is one other reason why people lie. And I know all too well about this one. People lie *because they are afraid*.

In Mark 14.66–72 NIV, we read the story of Peter's denial of Jesus Christ. 'I don't know or understand what you're talking about,' he declared to the servant girl who questioned him. He was afraid. He knew Jesus was about to die. And his trembling terror overcame his loyalty.

Fear is one of the main reasons people tell lies. These people know that lying is sin. They don't want to lie and they aren't really ready to lie. But when a horrible incident occurs, they start to fear. They are afraid of hardship and danger. And they want to escape. The simplest way for them to do so is to lie in order to elude the difficulties and dangers.

Peter was a strong and brave man. How could he be so weak and defeated? How can this not make people wonder? Isn't it strange?

No, it is not strange at all. When a Christian is in fear, he can tell any kind of lie if it will enable him to escape from danger. He will not admit to believing in God, in the Lord whom he serves. His heart may be thinking 'black' but his mouth will follow the others who are saying, 'Oh, this is white'.

This man will give false testimony, harming his friends. But afterwards he will not have peace in his heart. He will be very sad, and will even weep like Peter.

Our Lord will not rebuke this kind of believer very much because He knows that the person never intended to rebel against Him. It was only because he was afraid and weak that he fell. When His loving eyes are turned upon that sinner, he wants to repent. How could His wonderful love and gracious forgiveness not touch our hearts? He makes us want to live for Him and willingly die for Him, too.

So if you have committed a sin, confess and repent. After you fall and stand up again, keep moving forward. Just be extra careful of your footsteps, so you don't ever fall again.

If we want to eliminate the sin of lies, we should first eliminate the sin of greed. The sin of wanting a name. The sin of snatching power. The sin of hiding other sin. The sin of harming people. The sin of adultery.

And we must get rid of fear! Fear is a sin in itself. Fear doesn't trust God. If we fully honour and respect our Lord, believing in His great power, trusting in His faithfulness and love, we will fear nothing. No person, no accident, no disaster, no trouble, no danger at all can cause us to have fear. May we yield ourselves to know clearly and accept that fear is a sin.

Wang Ming-Tao stopped at this point. And as I looked at him, my eyes blurred with tears. *Here is a saint of God – a forgiven saint who knows very well what he is saying.*

'Uncle, do you really feel that fear is such a terrible sin?' I somehow wanted to lighten the burden of his past.

'Brother David, in the Bible, God doesn't only put all sins together, he puts the sin of fear before all others!'

'What do you mean?'

'I mean Revelation 21.8 NIV. "But the cowardly, the unbelieving, the vile, the murderers, the sexually immoral, those who practise magic arts, the idolaters and all liars — their place will be in the fiery lake of burning sulphur. This is the second death."'

We looked at each other for a moment before I spoke. 'So denial of the faith comes from fear . . . no matter what the danger.'

Wang Ming-Tao nodded. 'Denial springs from fear. Fear simply means we don't trust God.

'And fear is sin.'

8. Baptism by Fire

In Shanghai's harbour, gleaming white vessels glide gracefully past earth-hued junks with their quaint, quilted sails. Every day, hundreds of ships and thousands of boats chug their way along the Huangpu River waterfront. Only the city streets are more crowded.

Beside the harbour, along each avenue, a casual observer becomes enchanted by the sights and sounds of the ancient Oriental city. So many faces, so much movement. Ideological differences seem lost, locked away secretly behind the facade of jovial activity and bustling effort.

In the heart of Shanghai, however, lives an old man whose frail body bears witness to the physical reality of differing points of view. Wang Ming-Tao never complains. He never seems to consider reporting the price he has paid for his unfailing Christian perspective. And yet one knows far too much about him to forget, even for a moment, the outrageous abuse he has encountered.

Steaming tea refreshed us one afternoon as we talked of many things. As was often the case in our conversations, the subject soon turned to the plight of the Chinese Christian Church. 'Is there persecution here, Uncle? Tell me what you see . . .' The old man looked at his wife. Her face looked worried. 'Don't say anything else!' she silently cautioned him with her eyes. And he didn't.

But I knew that there were spiritual aspects of the subject he would feel free to share with me. 'What is the purpose of suffering? Talk to me about that . . .'

'Suffering edifies believers. It purifies them and helps them stay away from sin and unrighteousness. Suffering makes a way for Christians to become holy and perfect.'

Soon the old man was sharing another private sermon with me. And I knew, once again, that he spoke from experience as well as from understanding. He began by reciting a familiar Scripture:

> My son, despise not thou the chastening of the Lord, nor faint when thou art rebuked of Him: For whom the Lord loveth He chasteneth, and scourgeth every son whom He receiveth. If ye endure chastening, God dealeth with you as with sons; for what son is he whom the father chasteneth not? But if ye be without chastisement, whereof all are partakers, then are ye bastards, and not sons. Furthermore we have had fathers of our flesh which corrected us, and we gave them reverence: shall we not much rather be in subjection unto the Father of spirits, and live?
>
> For they verily for a few days chastened us after their own pleasure; but He for our profit, that we might be partakers of His holiness. Now no chastening for the present seemeth to be joyous, but grievous: nevertheless afterward it yieldeth the peaceable fruit of righteousness unto them which are exercised thereby. Wherefore lift up the hands which hang down, and the feeble knees; and make straight paths for your feet, lest that which is lame be turned out of the way; but let it rather be healed' (Heb. 12. 5–13 KJV).

Human nature loves ease and comfort. But God demands of us high virtue and perfect good deeds. He knows easy circumstances are not as conducive to our progress as suffering is; and He sees farther than our human eyes can look. God wants us to endure temporary and light affliction so that we may be sanctified and perfect, fit for the Master's use.

Fire is often used in the Bible to symbolize suffering, and very fitting it is. You know that gold and silver don't come from the mine pure and complete. When mined, they come as ore mixed with many impurities. They are neither beautiful to look at nor useful. But what do you do with the ore? Throw it away?

Of course not. People don't discard the ore because it is not pure and fine. What they do is put it into the fire. They refine it once, twice and even many, many times. The more harsh the refining process, the purer and finer the metal becomes. Finally it can be made into precious utensils of highest value and usefulness.

We believers are just like gold and silver in God's sight. God picked us out of the world for the purpose of making us into precious vessels. But because we had been buried in this corrupt and wicked society for so long, our hearts and minds were contaminated with impurities.

Our Lord doesn't discard us because of this. Instead He puts us in the crucible of affliction, to burn away the impurities. How painful and unbearable is the process! And in the course of this suffering, God causes us to confess and reject our personal sins. That way we learn to achieve the virtue God expects of us. Gradually we become perfect.

For this very reason, God has prepared a three-step baptism for His children. First they are baptized in water. Next in the Holy Spirit. Then in the fire.

Now water baptism and Spirit baptism are easy to understand. But what is baptism by fire? To understand this, read Luke 12.49–53 KJV 'I am come to send fire on the earth; and what will I, if it be already kindled? But I have a baptism to be baptized with; and how am I straitened till it be accomplished! Suppose ye that I am come to give peace on earth? I tell you, Nay; but rather division.'

The Lord Jesus said He came to cast fire on earth; and He added that He wanted to see it burn on. This is not easy to understand. Yet He continued to say that there was a baptism He must accept and He could not rest until it was over.

At the time He said this, Jesus had already received water baptism at the Jordan River. And as He came out of the water, He also received the Holy Spirit's baptism. What more baptism did He need? From John's testimony, we know that Jesus is going to baptize with the Holy Spirit and with fire. And this would not be only for others. He Himself must pass through the experience first.

'Suppose,' he asked, 'that I came to bring peace to the world? Not peace, I tell you, but division.' Here the Lord Jesus said plainly that to send fire on earth is to cause calamity, unrest, conflict, persecution and many afflictions to occur. And for what good purpose?

Our Lord does this because those who truly love and follow Him are not acceptable to the world. Sometimes they are opposed by their own households. Division arises even within families. Are these divisions good or bad? Of course they are good! For where there is division, the true disciples of the Lord are revealed. That is why, when speaking of this particular form of fire, our Lord Jesus said, 'How I wish it were already kindled!'

After considering this passage, we realize that the baptism by fire signifies suffering. The apostle Peter well understood this, and comforted his readers with these words: 'Beloved, think it not strange concerning the fiery trial which is to try you, as though some strange thing happened unto you: but rejoice, inasmuch as ye are partakers of Christ's sufferings;

that, when his glory shall be revealed, ye may be glad also with exceeding joy' (1 Pet. 4.12–13 KJV).

The baptism of water, the baptism of the Holy Spirit and baptism by fire. All three of these were submitted to by our Lord Jesus. His disciples must walk the path He walked so that they can also enter into His glory. When believers understand this, they'll never want to evade suffering!

There are two things that God wants to give to those who love Him. One is the Cross, and the other is the Crown. Everyone who hopes to obtain the Crown of Glory at Christ's appearing must take up the Cross of Suffering today.

But there is a comforting thought, and it is this. The Cross of Suffering is to be borne but for a few scores of years and will be completely obliterated at Christ's appearing. But the Crown which is given in exchange for the Cross remains forever.

'For which cause we faint not; but though our outward man perish, yet the inward man is renewed day by day. For our light affliction, which is but for a moment, worketh for us a far more exceeding and eternal weight of glory; while we look not at the things which are seen, but at the things which are not seen; for the things which are seen are temporal; but the things which are not seen are eternal' (2 Cor. 4.16–18 KJV).

Do you wish to obtain greater help and benefit, and greater grace from God? Then don't be afraid to suffer. God's grace and suffering are given together to those who love Him. We should not ask exemption from suffering, but should ask that God add to our faith and power to ensure and to derive benefits.

If you are in the midst of trials and tribulations now, don't look upon them as misfortunes. Don't assume that God has forsaken you. If that's what you think, you're mistaken. Remind yourself that suffering does not come without reason. Do not forget what the Bible says, 'All things work together for good to them that love God, to them who are called according to his purpose' (Rom. 8.28 KJV).

We should not worry about how heavy the burden, or how difficult the circumstances or how intense the pain. Instead we should simply say, Am I among those who love God? If we are, no matter what we encounter, God will use it to edify. To prune. To comfort. Our only duty is to learn to love God. He is faithful. He will not retract His promise. Take heart!

But heed a word of warning. The enemy is not happy to see God's children grow well. He knows that when they pass through suffering they become more apt to conquer. So he concentrates his attack in order to seduce those in the middle of the fire.

We believers, because of our fleshly weakness, are vulnerable to this subtle attack. With any slight wobbling of faith, Satan penetrates and makes the believer doubt, complain, rebel and reject God. He is even able to cause some to fall down entirely, straight into his devouring trap. To guard against this danger, remember the words of the Scripture.

'Casting all your care upon him; for he careth for you. Be sober, be vigilant; because your adversary the devil, as a roaring lion, walketh about, seeking whom he may devour: whom resist stedfast in the faith, knowing that the same afflictions are accomplished in your brethren that are in the world. But the God of all grace, who hath called us unto his eternal glory by Christ Jesus, after that ye have suffered a while, make you perfect, stablish, strengthen, settle you. To him be glory and dominion for ever and ever. Amen' (1 Pet. 5.7–11 KJV).

There he sat, the old warrior. Every word he spoke came from the very crucible he had just described. I recalled the sense of honour I felt in the presence of the seven believers I had been introduced to at Ping's house the day

I met Wang Ming-Tao. Now I felt even more privileged to have heard him speak so eloquently with regard to suffering.

It may be prison, I thought to myself. *It may be torture. It may be death. It could be subtle sarcasm from worldly friends. It might be the unkind judgment of other Christians who haven't taken the time to understand. A husband's rejection, a wife's indifference, the death of a child. Sickness or injury, loss or loneliness.*

Whatever the form human suffering takes, God's Word applies to it all . . .

'I wish my friends in America could hear your words the way I have, Uncle.'

He smiled joyfully. 'I pray every day for our brothers and sisters who live in freedom,' he told me. 'And this is my prayer:

'Lord, teach them not to love the world but to love the Word!'

Section V

His Song

'Onward, Christian soldiers.'

9. Another Perspective

A friend of Wang Ming-Tao, indeed a devoted friend
to suffering Christians worldwide, is renowned *Time*
correspondent David Aikman. During his two years as
Bureau Chief in Peking, David told me that he would
value the opportunity to meet Wang Ming-Tao. He was
interested professionally, of course. But as a Christian
believer, he also longed to have fellowship himself with
the man who had stood as a steel-reinforced pillar of
evangelical Christian truth for more than fifty years.

The meeting was arranged and finally took place in
1985. World-renowned journalist met world-famous pastor. Some time later, I was able to talk to David Aikman
about the time he spent with Wang Ming-Tao. We sat
in a pleasant diningroom in Washington, D.C., late one
afternoon, and he shared his thoughts with me.

'What did you think of him, David? What did you see
in his character?'

'I think the first thing that struck me about him was
the quality of having seen and experienced almost everything one can in life. Somehow he had worked out for
himself a way to filter those experiences successfully
through his Christian faith. Obviously, in his case, that
came about because of the intense suffering he faced during his prison years.

'This was not just physical suffering, but emotional
and psychological suffering as well. He had been able to
use that suffering to refine his character rather than to become bitter or resentful. And it had refined his character.

'There was a sort of bubbling undercurrent of joy in the man. It expressed itself in a very high level of humour. He seems very humorous. And it struck me that the humour was of a man who really was not capable any longer of being shocked or discomforted by the kind of harsh experiences that would really throw most of us for a loop.

'I suppose, to sum that all up, there was a sense of refinement, of spiritual refinement, in the most literal sense: the gold has been refined.'

I nodded, fully in agreement with his perspective. 'You'd never met him before, had you, David? So you didn't know him . . .'

'I had known of Wang Ming-Tao for a good decade or more before I met him. I knew who he was, I knew about him, I knew the basic background of his life. And when I met him I sensed that there wasn't a lot of Wang Ming-Tao that God still had to deal with. I got the feeling that God had a good old go with Wang and that Wang Ming-Tao willingly or otherwise had allowed it to happen and had come through it very well.

'The most profound impression that he made on me was actually at the point when we parted company after an hour and a half or two hours. Quite suddenly he got up—I was about to leave—and he and his wife began to sing "Onward, Christian soldiers". It struck me that the gesture wasn't phony. It wasn't designed to please me. It was the gesture of a man who wanted to reaffirm vigorously where his heart was.'

I recalled a similar experience with the old man. He had sung the same song for me, marching around the room like a youth. I chuckled at the memory. 'Did he tell you much about his prison experiences, David?'

'I think I asked him what he saw as the single most important lesson he'd derived from his imprisonment. What could the people in the West learn from his experiences? He simply said, "The Word. The Word."'

'That's exactly what he would say.'

'I think I'd been expecting a man with a lot to say. But he didn't really want to say a great deal.'

A professional historian, David Aikman is a man who knows Chinese history as well as anyone on earth.

'Wang Ming-Tao was born in 1900. Can you give me a brief sketch of what has happened in China since that year? What would this man have gone through?'

'Well – let me see . . . If he was born in 1900, that was the year of the Boxer Rebellion. The Boxer Rebellion epitomized Chinese grass roots frustration with Western control. The Western powers were determined not to allow violent rebellion in China to shake their interests in the country. The Chinese were reacting to that interference.'

I tried to review my own memory of Chinese history. 'What came next?'

'Wang would have been eleven when the Manchu dynasty was overthrown. So he would have experienced, in effect, eleven years under the imperial system of China which was introduced under the Qin dynasty emperor in the year 221 BC.

'He would have experienced the disillusionment of those who hoped for a genuine republican form of government after 1911. In reality China was divided into warlord fiefdoms. Then, as the central republican government did take power, it became corrupted from within. The administrators seemed to lose interest in the people's welfare.

'He would have experienced the first real hope of a unified China under a legitimate government in 1928 when the Nationalists marched north, beginning in 1926. This was under the leadership of Chiang Kai-Shek.'

'Sun Yat-Sen came before that – correct?'

'Yes. Sun Yat-Sen was responsible for overthrowing the Manchu dynasty, but he didn't really have any effective power until around 1920. Then he died in 1924.

'Wang Ming-Tao would have been aware, in his twenties, of the clash of ideas in China. In the twenties and thirties, all sorts of conflicting world views were struggling for recognition and supremacy. Of course this marked the beginning of the Marxist movement. The Chinese Communist Party was founded in 1921. Meanwhile, Western trained intellectuals were influenced by American notions of pragmatism – Thomas Dewey and so forth. A lot of people thought democratic liberalism would save China.'

'That's about the time the Japanese began their move into China.'

'That's right. During this period there was a great upsurge in Chinese patriotism. It was believed that if science were cultivated effectively and if democratic values were instituted in China, the country would kick itself out of its despondent, backward condition and join the ranks of the foremost nations of the world.

'But by the 1930s, a lot of these intellectual arguments had become sterile because the Japanese were demonstrating more powerfully than ever the impotence of China's government to keep its territory secure.

'Meanwhile, the Communists had developed what started off as an isolated insurrection in the south-eastern provinces into a well-organized major alternative form of government.'

I recalled the fact that Wang Ming-Tao's Peking Christian Tabernacle had been completed just as the Japanese invaded the city. 'How do you think the believers responded to all these changes?'

David shook his head. 'For men like Wang Ming-Tao, there must have been a lot of agonizing over the seeming inability of Christians to collectively influence the course of events. You have to bear in mind that the Christian role in China was disproportionately big in relation to the number of Christians around.

'We know, for example, that in 1949, the year of the Communist takeover, there were an estimated three million Roman Catholics and one million Protestants. The entire population of China was about 450 million. That's a tiny one per cent. Yet Christians had some very important positions in universities, in the military, in politics and in the arts. They were well represented in society as a whole. Yet they seemed to have very little influence on the social and political struggles taking place in China.'

'So for a man like Wang Ming-Tao, it must have raised a lot of questions. In any case, he probably would have felt that whatever happened politically, his job was to be an evangelist, to bring as many as possible into the kingdom of God.'

'Brother David, I'm sure that's the way he felt. Ironically, he was the one to establish the first Three-Self church in China—self-propagating, self-governing and self-supporting!'

'His church was the first Three-Self church, but it had nothing to do with the Three-Self Patriotic Movement. That's one reason he's so strongly against the Three-Self. Besides they're all tied into the Communist Party now.'

An amused expression flitted across David's face. 'Well, I'm sure he felt they didn't have anything to teach him about genuine self-government, genuine self-support and genuine self-propagation.'

I chuckled at the picture of Wang learning lessons from the Three-Self. 'Being a Chinese pastor in the early forties must have been quite a challenge.'

'Well, yes. You had the war between 1937 and 1945 when both the Nationalists and the Communists were fighting the Japanese. An evangelist at the time must have felt he was somewhat outside the main course of events. People were primarily concerned with the war and winning it. It would have been a frustrating period. But the worst was yet to come.'

'The civil war?'

'The civil war – one of the greatest civil wars of all time in any country. Millions of people were involved on each side. And Christians were forced to take choices that they never imagined they would have to take.

'Would they compromise with the victorious Communist regime? Would they flee to Taiwan with the Nationalists? Perhaps for many Chinese, Christianity came to be identified with the losing side, with a discredited political group. But would they stay and risk persecution? Maybe death?'

I thought about the old man on the other side of the world. 'He's really seen it all, hasn't he?'

'Well, of course, Wang Ming-Tao really grew up with the century in China. He saw the idealism of the very early 1950s when China was adopting a united front policy toward 'non-Communist patriots', as they called those who supported the revolution.

'He would have seen the increasing radicalization of China under Mao in the fifties. The increasing suspiciousness of Mao. This, naturally, made life very difficult for Christians. And Wang himself was caught up in the worst of that in 1957 with the campaign against the civil rightists.

'At that time, in 1957 and 1958, literally hundreds of thousands of Chinese intellectuals, Christians and others – especially those with Western training – were packed off to labour camps. And, in the case of Christians, they were forced to show approval of the government-sponsored Three-Self church.'

'If they didn't do that, how were they considered?'

'If they didn't co-operate with the Three-Self, they were considered little more than counter-revolutionaries. The Three-Self identified itself with the people. Therefore, anyone who didn't want to identify with the Three-Self movement was against the people. That meant that any Christian individual or organization which refused to be registered was counter-revolutionary. And that is a very, very serious offence in a Communist country.'

Our time together was drawing to a close. David Aikman was on his way back to the Washington, D.C., bureau of *Time* Magazine. I was within hours of returning to Hong Kong. I looked at my watch and shrugged.

'One last question, David. What does Wang Ming-Tao's life say to us today? What does it say to you?'

'It says many different things. First of all, God keeps His people even when His people let Him down. The other night I was reading in Timothy where a saying is quoted by Paul, 'If we deny him, he also will deny us: if we believe not, yet he abideth faithful: he cannot deny himself' (2 Tim. 2.12, 13).

'Now I never used to understand that, but I think what it means is that God expects us to acknowledge that we are His children, and that's the condition for His supporting us. To deny Him is to disown Him. On the other hand, He doesn't expect us to qualify as great masters of faith all the time.

'And He is faithful to us because if He weren't, He would not be true to His own character.

'The bottom line of Wang Ming-Tao's life is that God was faithful to him even though Wang Ming-Tao was, at times, not faithful to God. His life represents the faithfulness of God, in spite of his own unfaithfulness, in spite of his denial.

'And, as in the case of Anatoly Scharansky, the dissident Russian leader, it all demonstrates a relentless refusal to say that two plus two equals five or three.

'For all these years, Wang Ming-Tao has quietly gone on saying, "Two plus two equals four!"'

Section VI

His Victory

'There are many beginnings, but few endings.'

'Walk the hard road.'

Wang Ming-Tao

10. Only One Thing to Fear

The old man sits in his cushionless chair, a vase of chrysanthemums blazing brilliant-yellow beside him. On his left, a bookcase holds two dozen well-worn volumes. Behind him hang the beautiful, hand-brushed proverbs that provide the room's only real decoration.

His trousers are grey, his jacket dark-blue, and an old cap covers his thinning hair. As he speaks, his face becomes animated and radiant with joy. A tape-recorder rests atop the table where he and his wife eat.

No matter how harsh the winter, it is never cold in Wang's apartment. Along the wall is a charcoal heater that keeps the room pleasant and cosy. And the comfort of his guests is a very important thing to Wang Ming-Tao. That is made clear from the beginning.

Debra, his pretty wife, is always beside him as he speaks. Behind him is a window. And from the ceiling a bare bulb hangs, bathing the room in light by day or night.

Debra, Wang Ming-Tao and I sat visiting one afternoon in 1985. We had brought along my friend JE, and Eddie from New Zealand and a few other guests from America, and were enjoying a pleasant conversation with the two elders. All at once a man walked into the room, uninvited and unannounced.

Wang Ming-Tao never even hesitated. He went right on telling us his story as if nothing at all were happening. Debra looked nervously about, her eyes pleading with her husband to guard his words, to watch his tongue.

But Wang appeared oblivious to the situation.

Meanwhile, the people I had brought with me from Texas and Oklahoma were noticeably shocked. Prior to their visit with Wang, they had felt that a trip into China was more or less a holiday – and it might appear so to any tourist. People come and go as if no one were watching. To the casual observer, it appears that the Communist forces of darkness have no contact with the common people.

But after our visit to Wang's apartment, my American friends were thinking far different thoughts. When those men left China, they left with a personal understanding that the Church of Jesus Christ is still being very carefully watched by the Chinese.

During one afternoon in 1987, Eddie, Stephen, Sam and I visited Wang Ming-Tao. 'Do you have a message for the Church in the outside world?' I asked him.

He thought the question through for a moment, and then replied, 'In my long life I have known all kinds of trials and testings. Psalm 66 really describes all that I have been through. Verse 12 says, "We have passed through the waters and through the fire, but you cause us to come to a place of great abundance."

'I have been through fire and water. The water was deep and the fire blazing. But all these have passed away. Many times in the last twenty years I have come close to death. But each time I have passed safely through.

'My Lord has led me through the waters and through fire and now has brought me to a place of great abundance. All these things have been entirely to my good. "And we know that all things work together for good to them that love God, to them who are the called according to his purpose" (Rom. 8.28 KJV).

'I have suffered many serious illnesses. In 1961 through 1962, I was desperately ill, lying flat out on my bed for a whole year, spitting blood. Would I have said at that time that I was going to live? But God performed a miracle. After an entire year, He healed me completely.

Two years or so after that, I had an X-ray taken which showed that there was no trace of the disease and that the damaged portions of the lung were already renewed.

'After that came many other trials and evils—things that are not easy for tongue to describe. But thanks be to God, He has caused my faith (apart from that one point where I wavered) to stand firm to the end. He has restored the faith I had more than twenty-five years ago. As a matter of face, He has strengthened that faith so that it is firmer now than it was before.

'From this, I can now understand that God's way of working within the lives of those whom He loves is truly wonderful. The experiences I remember best are those that revealed God's presence. His power. His wisdom and His grace.

'To speak of all these things would take longer than just an hour . . . longer than even a thousand hours.

'To summarize it all is to say simply that God has allowed me to go through many trials and adversities, all of them to test and refine me. He has done this so that in the end I might be stronger than ever, more pure-hearted, more loyal toward my God.

'I remember the words of Jesus to His church as recorded in Revelation 2.10 KJV, "Fear none of those things which thou shalt suffer: behold, the devil shall cast some of you into prison, that ye may be tried; and ye shall have tribulation ten days; be thou faithful unto death, and I will give thee a crown of life."

'So I encountered twenty-two years and ten months of refining and the Lord has not allowed me to suffer any loss at all. Instead I have received the greatest of blessings.

'An ancient Chinese proverb says, "There are many beginnings, but few endings." Every person who attempts to do something in this world makes a start. But those who carry through to the end and complete the task are very few.'

As I left Wang Ming-Tao, I thought again of his extraordinary life. To our own generation, he represents two thousand years of Christian faithfulness, even to the point of death. Century after century, nation after nation has seen suffering on behalf of the Lord Jesus Christ.

A familiar Scripture came into my mind. 'Therefore, since we have so great a cloud of witnesses surrounding us, let us also lay aside every encumbrance, and the sin which so easily entangles us, and let us run with endurance the race that is set before us, fixing our eyes on Jesus, the author and perfecter of faith, who for the joy set before him endured the cross, despising the shame, and has sat down at the right hand of the throne of God' (Heb. 12.1–2 NAS).

The orange and white bus carried me back to my hotel. In the streets around me, thousands of unknown Chinese went about their business, caught up in the daily routine of their lives. Like men and women everywhere, they had their own fears. Their personal triumphs. Their heartbreaking disappointments.

'Many beginnings, few endings.' So the old man had said.

For the Christian believer, that Chinese saying bears a sobering message. Wang Ming-Tao had chosen to follow Jesus. In the face of adversity he had turned back. Only God's forgiveness had restored him to a new beginning.

When confronted with pain and probable death, Wang had failed. So often we are simply confronted with life. Death or life. Which is more terrifying?

I thought of him, sitting victoriously there in his little apartment. He is a totally free man. He has nothing on earth to lose. Today, in the mind of Wang Ming-Tao, there is only one thing to fear – DENIAL.

As I left him, I had turned and asked a final question. 'Uncle, do you have any precious lessons to share with the Christians in free countries?'

I can still see him, framed in the simple doorway,

his nearly-blind eyes focused on my face. He nodded, beginning to close the door as he answered me.

'Tell them,' he replied, a gentle smile at his lips, 'to walk the hard road.'

ADDTIONAL BOOKS RECOMMENDED
FOR READING

Adeney, David, *China: The Church's Long March* (Regal Books, Ventura, CA 1985)

Brother David, *God's Smuggler to China* (Hodder and Stoughton, London 1983)

Butterfield, Fox, *China, Alive in the Bitter Sea*

Chang, Nien, *Life and Death in Shanghai* (Grove Press, 1987)

Lawrence, Carl, *The Church in China: How it Survives and Prospers Under Communism* (Bethany House Publishers, Minneapolis, MN 1985)

'Massacre in Beijing: China's Struggle for Democracy' in *Time* magazine (Warner Books 1989)

National Geographic Society, *Journey Into China* (National Geographic Society, Washington D.C. 1982)

Wallis, Arthur, *China Miracle* (Kingsway Publications, East Sussex 1985)

For research on China and regular reports:

The Chinese Church Research Centre
7 Kent Road, Flat A
Kowloon, Hong Kong

Overseas Missionary Fellowship
P.O. Box 70505
Kowloon Central Post Office
Kowloon, Hong Kong

For direct involvement through literature and other materials:

Asian Outreach
G.P.O. 3448
Hong Kong

Christian Communications, Ltd.
P.O. Box 95364 Tsimshatsui
Kowloon, Hong Kong

Open Doors with Brother Andrew
16520 Harbor Blvd. Suite G
Fountain Valley, CA 92708

World Home Bible League
16801 Van Dam Road
South Holland, IL 60473

To sponsor or produce radio programs for China:

Far East Broadcasting Associates
P.O. Box 9–6789 Tsimshatsui
Kowloon, Hong Kong

Trans World Radio
10th Floor On Lee Bldg.
Kowloon, Hong Kong

For involvement with the church in North Korea:

Cornerstone Ministries
P.O. Box 27188
Los Angeles, CA 90027